CURAT

HISTORIC ROYAL PALACES

HISTORIC ROYAL PALACES

SCALA

INTRODUCTION

EACH OF THE five royal palaces in our care has survived a chequered history spanning hundreds of years. They have witnessed peace and prosperity, along with splendid periods of building and expansion, but they also share stories of war and domestic strife, politics and revolution. The Tower of London, one of the world's most famous fortresses, is notorious as a place of torture and execution, but it has also been an opulent royal palace, and at various times housed an armoury, the Royal Mint and even a zoo! Hampton Court Palace, where Henry VIII lavished money on fabulous tapestries and entertainments, was partially rebuilt in grand style for William III by Sir Christopher Wren and his clerk of works, Nicholas Hawksmoor. The original ambitious plan to replace the Tudor palace was modified when funds were found to be lacking, and only the king's and queen's apartments were rebuilt. As a result, today we enjoy two palaces – Tudor and Baroque – for the price of one. Kensington Palace, built in 1689 as a royal retreat, is probably most famous as the birthplace and childhood home of Queen Victoria. It is here that the 18-year-old princess was awoken on 20 June 1837 to learn that she was queen. Kew Palace was part of the summer 'country house' retreat used by George III, Queen Charlotte and some of their 15 children. It was a place of laughter, music and family picnics in the nearby Queen Charlotte's Cottage – until the mood darkened. The king, stricken by his 'madness', was incarcerated in the palace, while Charlotte kept their eldest daughters close by her for comfort, the girls' youth and marriage prospects fading all the while.

THIS PAGE:
Hampton Court Palace
OPPOSITE (FROM TOP):
The *Tower of London*,
Kew Palace, the *Banqueting House* and *Kensington Palace*

And the Banqueting House is the standing survivor of the vast and vanished Whitehall Palace, and was the scene of the execution of King Charles I in 1649.

The palaces' contents – by turns exquisite, intriguing, quirky – echo these distinguished histories. Examples of superb craftsmanship stand alongside hastily built structures that were never designed to stand the test of time (but somehow have). Everyday objects – a child's toy, a tankard – rank among prestigious artworks and precious jewels, survivors all of momentous times and famous (and sometimes infamous) owners.

Eleven of our curators – Sally Dixon-Smith, Brett Dolman, Meg Dorman, Sebastian Edwards, Susanne Groom, Alexandra Kim, Deirdre Murphy, Lee Prosser, Kent Rawlinson, Jane Spooner and Chief Curator, Lucy Worsley (identified by their initials in the text) – have each chosen objects that excite them and that speak particularly to them. Their expert knowledge and skill in studying these buildings and their contents brings to life the stories of the people who have lived and worked in the palaces; and they are inspired by the most commonplace relics from the past as well as the most glorious. Some items are so fragile and light-sensitive that they cannot be exposed on permanent display; others are so precious that they can be seen only by special arrangement. Our curators open the door on some of these hidden riches, along with the many items on public display that can be enjoyed by all visitors to the palaces.

This is a collection of personal responses to some of the objects that have been offered up over nine centuries of history, craftsmanship and art. We warmly invite you to explore these magnificent palaces and discover their stories for yourself.

The Byward Tower wall painting, 14th century

Oil paint and gilding on plaster and stone
180 x 414 cm
BYWARD TOWER, TOWER OF LONDON (view by special arrangement)

IN 1953, WORKERS renovating rooms for Yeoman Warder lodgings stripped out a Victorian hearth to reveal a decorated Tudor fireplace. A painting conservator took a closer look at the medieval wall behind it and discovered an astonishing fourteenth-century mural under seven layers of limewash. It was a big news story at the time: these are royal wall paintings of the highest quality, and are extremely rare survivals. The scene is of two saints flanking the Crucifixion, although the central image of Christ on the Cross was destroyed when Tudor builders punched a hole in the wall for their fireplace. The 'International Gothic' style of the figures – with soft facial features, large noses and sweet expressions – combined with the presence of his patron saint, St John the Baptist, indicate that the murals were produced in the 1390s for Richard II. They are painted in expensive pigments, including a red made from the secretions of insects' larvae. On the far left St John the Baptist carries the Lamb of God; next to him the Virgin Mary wrings her hands in grief. To the right of the lost Crucifix is St John the Evangelist, then the splendid St Michael the Archangel, weighing the souls of the dead. Tiny devils try to weigh down his scales in favour of sending the souls to Hell. The background copies fourteenth-century Italian silk designs,

and is a vivid green with gilded heraldic lions, fleur-de-lys and collared parakeets. I think these exquisite paintings are so special because they present such a different view of the Tower of London, contrasting with its reputation as a place of brutality and torture. St Michael's beauty reminds us that the Tower was also a sumptuous palace with richly gilded paintings adorning its walls. JS

Court dress, 1920

JEANNE LANVIN 1867–1946
Silk
KENSINGTON PALACE (on rotating display)

WE HOLD AN AMAZING collection of female Court dress at Kensington Palace from the past 250 years; gorgeous, costly gowns designed to be worn in the presence of royalty. In the eighteenth century, the mantua was worn exclusively at Court: an antiquated style of dress, it was a preposterous size (see pages 50–51) and made from such luxurious fabric that it effectively excluded from Court anyone not wealthy enough to own one. In the nineteenth century, the Lord Chamberlain produced a list of formal guidelines, stating that women were obliged to wear an evening gown with a full train and an ostrich feather headdress when being presented to the monarch. The 1920s heralded an altogether more modern approach. It was the Jazz Age; evening dresses were made short for dancing, and this became the style for attendances at Court also. But regulations still applied, and what is so delightful about the twentieth-century Court dresses is that they reflect so well the tensions between the conformity of Court and the seductions of style. This exquisite creation was designed by Jeanne Lanvin for Helen Wardman, the socialite daughter of a US architect, who wore it to

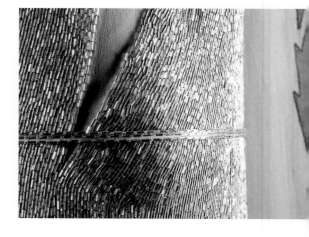

be presented at Court around 1928. The train would have been attached for her presentation to the king and queen – regulations stated that this must extend 18 inches along the ground, no more – and Helen would have had to wear ostrich feathers in her hair. But the gown itself is completely of the moment: made for dancing, it is really light and would move and shake with the wearer. I like to think that Helen, after 'coming out' at Court, might have removed the train, ditched the feathers and hit the town! DM

Triumph of Fame over Death from Petrarch's *Triumphs, c.*1515–20

Tapestry, wool and silk, 406 x 800 cm
Southern Netherlands
GREAT WATCHING CHAMBER, HAMPTON COURT PALACE

THIS VAST, COMPLICATED and beautiful tapestry is one of three that survives from an original set of six, once in the collection of Thomas Wolsey, then passed to Henry VIII. It is also an intriguing puzzle: over 200 figures from history and legend crowd the tapestry, but only a few are identified with little pieces of woven text. Each time I walk through the Great Watching Chamber, I stop to see if I can recognise any more. The story portrayed in the tapestries is a fourteenth-century morality tale by the Italian poet, Petrarch. The 'Triumphs' are those of Love; of Chastity over Love; of Death over Chastity; of Fame over Death; of Time over Fame; and Faith, or Eternity, over Time. In each tapestry, a victorious figure rides on a chariot in a grand procession, echoing the real-life triumphal processions of medieval Italy, in which figures representing Virtues conveyed dramatic messages to the watching population on how to live a good life. In a Court context, these tapestries served to illustrate good moral conduct for courtiers. In the left hand chariot of this tapestry is Atropos, representing Death, and in the triumphal chariot on the right, a beautiful woman with a trumpet (pictured), representing Fame. Put simply, the message is that if you live a heroic life you will be remembered after you die, thus Fame triumphs over Death. Conse-quently, the rest of the tapestry is filled with famous figures from history rising from their graves, summoned by a trumpeting Fame to live again. In another weaving of this tapes-try, now in the Victoria & Albert Museum, Wolsey had little portraits of himself and Henry VIII inserted among the heroic figures from the past. BD

The Hampton Court Maze, 17th century, re-presented 2005

Hornbeam
<small>HAMPTON COURT PALACE</small>

THE MAZE HAS almost legendary status as a place of mystery and intrigue. It is the only surviving part of what was originally a much bigger 'wilderness' garden, a place for the late Stuart courtiers to flirt discreetly with each other once out of sight and sound of their colleagues. Considering what a crowded place the Court was, full of eavesdroppers and backstabbers, the Maze must have been a liberating place to escape to. Jerome K. Jerome's book, *Three Men in a Boat*, tells the story of some visitors to Hampton Court who decide to 'pop into' the Maze before lunch one day. Needless to say they are trapped for several hours, and in the end 'had to wait for one of the old keepers to come back from his dinner before they could get out'. A few years ago, we decided to re-plant the Maze in its original hornbeam. It had been re-planted in yew in the twentieth century because yew is hardy and it made the hedge more 'visitor proof' (although most visitors are not as raucous as the schoolchildren in this whimsical London Transport poster of 1956!). Hornbeam has much more subtle, ethereal, beautiful leaves. In order to try and slow people down on their journey through the maze, a sound sculpture was also installed. Hidden speakers play a series of strange sounds throughout the Maze: silks rustle, bells ring, dogs bark – and fragments of poetry are read by people associated with the palace. I am quite proud to say that my own voice can be heard (saying 'salacious', as it happens). I have become a tiny part of the Maze myself. LW

A harassed school teacher from Hayes
Took her children to Hampton Court Maze,
They got thoroughly lost
At a moderate cost
And then had a wonderful time admiring
the Great Vine and imagining Henry VIII
serving double faults on the Tennis Court.
It was easy to get there, too — Green Line
Coaches 716, 716A, 718 and 725 run to the gates.

The Wolsey Closet, 16th century, with 19th century additions

Oil on panel
HAMPTON COURT PALACE

THE WOLSEY CLOSET is probably my favourite room in the palace, being almost the only place where one has a true sense of the intimacy and richness of the Tudor private apartments. It is a fragmentary part of Henry VIII's own 'privy chambers', almost all of which have been destroyed. It is also an intriguing puzzle, as it is unclear how much of the original room survives, and how much was pieced back together in the nineteenth century from both original and reconstructed elements. Although this was part of Henry's apartments, it is Wolsey's gilded motto (possibly added in the nineteenth century and thus adding to the confusion) that runs around the walls and gives the closet its name. The motto reads: DOMINUS MIHI ADIUTOR – The Lord is my helper. The paintings of the Passion Cycle, Christ's last few days on earth, show the astonishing quality of work that was being installed in Henry's palaces at this time. They may be by the Italian artist, Toto del Nunziata: we know from original accounts that he painted similar panels for some of Henry's other rooms. The linenfold panelling is not original, but it would have looked similar and was probably richly painted and gilded. With a wonderful patterned carpet and finely carved furniture, this room would have been a retreat where Henry could relax, read or entertain close companions. For me, the most astonishing part of the room is the ceiling. The finely decorated panels look like wood, plaster or stone but are in fact leather mâché – scraps of waste leather bound into a thick paste, pressed into a carved mould and left to dry. The resulting casts – flexible and light – could be nailed onto wooden backboards, painted with expensive blue (bice) pigment and gilded. The joints are hidden with wooden battens, and gilded lead leaves cover the corners. Beautiful! KR

Paper fashion doll and costumes, 18th century

Watercolour
Height 12.5 cm
KENSINGTON PALACE (not on display)

WHAT WAS THE FUNCTION of this beautifully drawn figure from the 1780s? Like today's paper dolls, her dresses have fold-over tabs to enable outfit changes, and the hats have a slit to allow them to sit properly on her fashionably frizzed hair. Yet these delicate little outfits seem too fragile for play. One possibility is that this doll was an early tool for communicating fashion ideas. Often dressmakers would use dolls, perfectly kitted out in miniature dress, as a way of exchanging the latest designs between themselves and with clients. What I find most appealing about this diminutive figure is how her paper wardrobe – from her riding habit to her grand Court dress and the everyday muslin frocks – provides such a wonderful insight into the fashions of the day. It is particularly exciting that the accessories that complete the outfits – hats, bags and headdresses – are included, as so often these ephemeral items don't survive. This paper doll was created in 1787 by Harriet Johnson, who came from a very fashion-aware family; her aunt was Barbara Johnson, whose wonderful book of eighteenth-century fabric samples and fashion plates is now in the Victoria & Albert Museum. The 14-year-old Harriet's regular correspondence with her aunt included lively anecdotes about parties, dinners and trips, and it is likely they spent many hours together discussing the latest trends. Both Barbara's fashion book and Harriet's paper doll were passed down the family together, and we were able to buy the doll at auction. It is wonderfully ironic that it should be this fragile paper representation that has survived to reveal to us what a stylish young thing of the 1780s would have been wearing. AK

The Triumphs of Caesar: canvas II ('The Triumphal Carts'), 1484–1505

ANDREA MANTEGNA *c.*1430–1506

Oil on canvas, 266 x 278 cm

THE LOWER ORANGERY, HAMPTON COURT PALACE

THRILLING BUT OFTEN OVERLOOKED, this set of canvases pres-
ents a challenge in that the once glorious colours have faded
and it can be hard to appreciate just how grand, original and
archaeologically accurate they are. To appreciate Mantegna's
achievement we should remember that secular painting on
this scale was unknown at this time; Michelangelo had not yet
attempted the Sistine Chapel ceiling, and Hollywood's ubiq-
uitous depictions of ancient Rome were centuries ahead.
Mantegna was immersed in the art, literature and architecture of ancient Rome. He used his knowledge and his mastery
of portraiture and perspective to make these paintings the
most authentic synthesis of a Roman triumph (the glorious
procession through the streets of Rome granted to a victorious general) ever attempted. Commissioned by the Marquis
of Mantua probably in about 1484, and bought by Charles I in
1629 for the Royal Collection, *The Triumphs* caused a sensation. The best way to experience them is to imagine yourself in
ancient Rome, with Julius Caesar's triumph rolling past as
people cheer. All around is noise and chaos; drums roll and
trumpets blare. The Roman army marches by, banners flying.
Their triumphal carts, pulled by straining elephants and oxen,
are loaded with the spoils of war: looted artefacts, vases
brimming with gold coins, armour ripped from defeated sol-
diers, statues smashed from buildings, captured kings and
queens and their enslaved, exhausted subjects. The ingenious
worm's-eye viewpoint makes you look upwards, allowing
Mantegna an economy of detail. There is no sea of monoto-
nous 'extras'; here, everyone is distinct, in motion, gesturing,
talking. In fact it is impossible to do justice to these paintings
with mere words. Come to the Lower Orangery and experience them for yourself! BD

Queen Victoria's small diamond crown, 1870

R & S GARRARD & COMPANY
Diamonds set in silver, laminated with gold
Height 9.4 cm, diameter at base 9 cm, weight 159 g
THE JEWEL HOUSE, TOWER OF LONDON

THIS EXQUISITE CROWN is the smallest in the collection. It looks almost like
a child's crown, but it was worn a great deal by Queen Victoria in her later
years and has become closely associated with her. She wears it in paintings, official photographs and sculptures, and on gold and silver coins.
Its delicacy – over 1,000 diamonds, clear set for maximum sparkle into a
fine openwork frame – was much appreciated by Victoria, a small woman
who found her large, heavy crown set with coloured stones exhausting
to wear. But this glittering miniature crown was commissioned not out
of pleasure, but from grief. When Prince Albert died of typhoid in 1861,
the heartbroken Victoria clad herself in mourning dress and withdrew
from public life completely. After several years, her absence was too much
for even the most sympathetic subject to bear, and public protest forced
the queen to re-enter the fray. So, while declaring her intention to wear
black for the rest of her life, Victoria had a suitable crown made to wear on
state occasions. Diamonds were a 'colourless' compromise, appropriate
for mourning. The crown's arches are removable, a clever design ele-
ment which allows the crown to be worn also as a circlet. All Queen
Consorts' crowns were made this way after this time, so that royal women
could wear their crowns less formally as jewellery. This tiny crown
demonstrates wonderfully how the grieving queen attempted to recon-
cile personal tragedy with her public-facing role: she would continue to do
her duty as Sovereign, but she would never forget Albert. SDS

The Apotheosis of King James I (detail), 1634

PETER PAUL RUBENS 1577–1640

Oil on canvas, 975 x 625 cm

THE BANQUETING HOUSE, WHITEHALL

WRITTEN ON THE FACE of my watch is a quotation from Baudelaire, '*L'air est plein du frisson des choses qui s'enfuient*', which, roughly translated, is 'The air is filled with echoes of the past'. I look at it several times a day, and nowhere evokes the sentiment of those words more forcefully than here, gazing up at the central section of this Rubens painting, which is so packed full of action that it looks as though it is moving upwards into the very heavens it depicts. Standing in this spot combines the joy of looking at this rich painting with the frisson of knowing this is where, in the seventeenth century, a visiting ambassador would stop to make his deepest reverence to the king, who simultaneously would descend the steps of the throne dais at the end of the hall to greet him.

The magnificent Rubens painting itself is a *tour de force* of symbolic illusion, as James I is carried on the back of an imperial eagle from his throne on earth to a christo-mythological throne in heaven, the whole echoing the words of the Stuart belief in the divine right of kings, that 'even on earth kings are called gods'. The paintings were commissioned by Charles I in 1630. Nineteen years later, the doomed king was to walk under this magnificent ceiling for the last time on his way to his execution. He must have looked upwards for one final glance at his father, James I, making his easy ascent to heaven, and for a second wondered how he would face his own very different journey to the final reckoning which was then awaiting him one step outside this room on the scaffold. Could any place be more *plein du frisson*? SG

Apollo Gazing at the Sun, 1996–2000, from a 17th-century original

Carrara marble
Privy Garden, Hampton Court Palace

WE HAVE TWO sculptures of *Apollo Gazing at the Sun* at the palace: this one is a copy of the Baroque original that stands in the Orangery, now too weather-damaged to survive outside. I find both of them wonderful. Apollo's four marble companions were re-carved for the restoration of William III's Privy Garden in 1995, but the re-carving of Apollo was delayed for what we hoped would be no longer than a year after that. The seventeenth-century statues were almost certainly made in Italy, shipped from Livorno and offered for sale to William III. They first appeared in the garden at Kensington Palace but were soon brought to Hampton Court. However, the king made no decision about them, reluctant either to pay the asking price of £600 or to return them to their owner, before he suddenly died in 1702. It is curious that Apollo is gazing due north, towards the palace, which is the wrong direction for him to be shielding his eyes from the sun! I think it might well be a private joke between kings. Apollo, the sun god, represents William's great adversary, Louis XIV, *le roi soleil* of France. The French king is dazzled not by the sun but by the magnificence of William's new palace, besides which Versailles pales into insignificance! Neil Simmons, the sculptor, and I share a private Apollo joke, too. It is customary to place a new coin on the pedestal beneath a statue when installing it. As Apollo was finally lowered into place on 4 April 2000 – four years late – Neil slipped a little note onto the plinth instead. In years to come, puzzled contractors may find it and read: 'Without the constant nagging of Mrs Groom this statue would never have been completed!' SG

Portrait of Princess Mary Stuart, 1637

ANTHONY VAN DYCK 1599–1641

Oil on canvas, 136.5 x 108.6 cm

HAMPTON COURT PALACE

MARY, THE ELDEST daughter of Charles I and Henrietta Maria, is five or six years old in this disarming portrait. Van Dyck had painted her several times before this – as a babe in arms and a toddler with her siblings – but here she is alone, dressed as a miniature adult in expensive silver lace, with pearls around her neck and in her hair. Her apron is her dresser's only concession to childhood. She is almost certainly being presented for the international marriage market. The late 1630s were not a good time for King Charles, who was spending too freely and ruling without Parliament, and a king's eldest daughter, no matter how tender her years,

was a valuable 'asset' to secure a political ally in Europe. Mary's little figure stands against a swathe of golden damask (one of the regular props in Van Dyck's dressing-up box), almost overwhelmed by the great column meant to emphasise her status. The portrait is rather stiff, yet there is the liveliness of early years in her face and hands. Close examination of this painting has revealed how Van Dyck typically worked, changing the hands to achieve the right expressive gesture. His formula worked; a few years later a worthy suitor was found. At the age of 12, Mary was married to the future Prince William II of Orange, in London, later joining him in the Netherlands. On their official 'wedding night', the very young couple lay next to one another in the presence of 'all the great Lords and Ladies of England', before William went off to his own chambers. He later said, 'although we were at first very solemn towards each other, now we feel more at ease: I find her to be more beautiful than the painting'. I like to think it was this portrait he was referring to, as it comes originally from the Dutch royal collection. SE

Hew Draper's graffito, 16th century

Stone carving
56 x 48 cm
SALT TOWER, TOWER OF LONDON

IN MARCH 1560, an apparently respectable and wealthy Bristol innkeeper, Hew Draper, was sent to the Tower accused of sorcery against two courtiers. Hew pleaded not guilty, although he admitted having dabbled in the past then burning his sorcerers' books in disgust. However, once incarcerated he set about carving a mysterious chart into the walls of his cell. This was possibly not the most prudent action for a suspected sorcerer, but Hew left behind a highly unusual – and mystifying – piece of prisoner graffito. A large amount of graffiti has been carved at the Tower over the centuries. Some of the wealthier inmates probably hired stonemasons to come in and chisel a bespoke rendition of their name or a suitably pious verse, while others wiled away the hours scratching initials or simple Christian symbols. But not Hew. We think he created this beautifully precise and skilful graffito himself. It carries the inscription: HEW DRAPER OF BRISTOW [Bristol] MADE THYS SPHEER THE 30 DAYE OF MAYE, ANNO 1561. But what does the sphere symbolise? It is a zodiac wheel with the different signs running anti-clockwise around it, and it looks as if it was created using a compass. I have established that the large grid is a chart of the days of the week and hours of the day, so at any given moment it is possible to see which planet is in the ascendant. Another intriguing aspect is that the graffito is situated low down on the wall. In the same month he dated the inscription, Hew was noted as being 'verie sicke', and after this the records fall silent. Did he carve this elaborate map of the heavens lying down, perhaps to distract himself from the pain of a mortal illness? SDS

Princess Elizabeth's painted picnic room, *c.*1804

Mural, oils

Queen Charlotte's Cottage (built 1770), Kew Gardens

Princess Elizabeth, the third and most artistic daughter of King George III and Queen Charlotte, created this mural in her mother's *cottage orné*. The beautifully conceived pattern of climbing bamboo, with its blue convolvulus and orange nasturtiums vibrant on their dark green painted foliage, creates the impression of standing beneath a flowery bower. I find it especially appealing for what it reveals about Elizabeth. She wished passionately to marry and have a home of her own to decorate. She jokingly described herself as a 'Cottager' in a letter to her brother, the Prince of Wales, in which she thanked him for sending her a present to enhance the 'dear little Cottage' she had obtained for herself at Windsor.

George III, who adored all his daughters, was loath to lose them to European princes in loveless diplomatic alliances. When Elizabeth was 18 years old, her father began his battle with his alarming illness, reluctantly and wrongly diagnosed by his physicians as dementia, and the Queen increasingly needed her daughters around her for help and support. As the three eldest princesses moved into their 30s, their marriage prospects had already dwindled considerably. Trapped, Elizabeth threw her energies into refurbishing the little cottage at Kew. In 1805, she invited both her parents to see the finished results, but a heavy shower of rain prevented the visit. It is possible that George III never saw the newly decorated room, as his illness worsened and he rarely visited Kew after 1806. Just before her mother's death in 1818, Princess Elizabeth escaped to marry the Prince of Hesse-Homborg. She was 49 years old. Still hoping for a family she took a layette with her, but it never came into use. I can imagine the princess here in this room, painting these beautiful flowers and dreaming of a romantic life in a little cottage of her own. SG

Carved keystone grotesques, *c.*1689

GRINLING GIBBONS 1648-1721

Portland stone

FOUNTAIN COURT CLOISTERS, HAMPTON COURT PALACE

THE ENGLISH NEVER really took to the heavy swirls, layers and wedding-cake detail that was so popular on the Continent during the period when Baroque architecture was in vogue. It was adopted, but with a more restrained and sober interpretation: 'less is more' was true, even then. Yet some choice touches can be found here and there, and these heads are about as exuberant as they come. They are also special as rare examples of Grinling Gibbons's carving in stone. Gibbons was said to be the greatest carver of his age, and his fantastic, meticulous limewood carvings can be found in many royal palaces, but not so often in stone. These keystones, from the arches around the cloister in Fountain Court, derive from a long tradition dating back to the medieval period, which we often recognise as 'green men' on ancient churches, with foliage sprouting from their mouths and ears, or with grimacing facial expressions. They come as a surprise, and have a liveliness that suggests the mason was given free rein with his imagination rather than being presented with a design and asked to copy it. The figures probably represent gods and goddesses, symbols of fertility and spirits of the forest. But there is also a more subtle meaning: cornucopias (horns of plenty), baskets bursting with fruit and flowers, cherubs' heads and heavenly trumpets were intended to convey that William and Mary had brought abundance and plenty to the kingdom. Grotesque they are, but not in a frightening way, more in the old-fashioned sense of the word, offering as they do a glimpse into the creativity and humour of the masons and carvers of the time. LP

Princess Charlotte of Mecklenburg-Strelitz, *c.*1761

JOHANN GEORG ZIESENIS 1716–1776

Oil on canvas, 134.9 x 96.8 cm

KING'S LIBRARY, KEW PALACE

CHARLOTTE, WHO BECAME George III of England's queen, is presented here as the epitome of the fairytale princess. She has the jewels, an exquisite gown, youth and beauty, and a romantic castle in the background. George III was smitten by this portrait. Admittedly, as it was probably painted as a pre-wedding gift for the king (that's his miniature in her lovely pearl bracelet), it gives a rather flattering impression. Lord Harcourt, sent to collect the princess from her little-known principality, describes her 'very pretty eyes', but comments she is 'no regular beauty'. I find this painting charming because it shows Charlotte at a happy time in her life, with much to live for – a foretaste of the king and queen's early golden years raising a young family during summers they spent at Kew. The contrast with portraits painted later in Charlotte's life is stark, and very moving. By 1789, her hair has turned white through the distress of losing two of her infant children, the traumas of her husband's alarming illness, diagnosed as dementia by 18th-century physicians, and the terrifying threat posed by the French Revolution. But here she is just 17, full of hope and expectation, dreaming of her life ahead. After this portrait was painted, things started moving quickly, but the hand of fate slowed the rapid course of events. Charlotte's mother died, delaying the princess's arrival in England, which was further impeded by severe storms at sea. She finally met the king in the garden of St James's Palace, and they fell in love. That same evening, Charlotte was dressed in her wedding gown, the bodice of which was so heavy with diamonds that it kept slipping down, so that when she arrived at the altar, 'the spectators knew as much of her upper half as the King himself'. Two weeks later, on 22 September 1761, Charlotte was crowned queen of England. SG

Georgian kitchen block, 1728–31

KEW PALACE

THE KEW KITCHEN – vast, atmospheric and practically untouched since 1818 – is an extraordinarily rare survival. Back in the 1730s, it hummed with life, with a bustling staff of around 30 labouring to prepare food for Frederick, Prince of Wales (father of George III), and other members of the royal family on their visits to his palatial mansion known as the White House, which stood nearby. Most other surrounding buildings – a stable block, dovecote and laundry – have long since disappeared, along with the mansion, which was pulled down in 1802, but by some quirk of fate the kitchen has survived. When Queen Charlotte died in 1818, the officials of the royal household simply locked the door and departed, and the kitchen was left untouched for almost 200 years. Remarkably, not only do the rooms survive, with their many original fixtures and fittings, including a massive oak table, but also an archive of documents detailing equipment that was bought, food that was served and the staff employed. We know that Charles Hamelton was the Clerk of the Kitchen in 1735, and he was supported by a large team, including three 'boys in the kitchen' who were probably responsible for the most menial tasks. Some of the furniture remains as it was left, including the copper  boilers and the charcoal stoves. Where other fixtures have disappeared, their ghostly outlines are still visible on walls, or in tiny fragments, and it is possible to see where shelves once sat, where ironwork held objects in place and where the kitchen clock used to hang. When the kitchen opens to the public in 2011, it is these details that will create a sense of the activity that once filled these rooms. The kitchen continues to yield treasures; we found an early nineteenth-century bathtub that may have been used by the ailing George III, who, it is recorded, took his medicinal baths in a room off the main kitchen, to spare his servants the bother of carrying heavy buckets of water across to Kew Palace. LP

Tijou screen, 1690

JEAN TIJOU *fl.* 1689–1712
Wrought iron
PRIVY GARDEN, HAMPTON COURT PALACE

THE TIJOU SCREEN is a passion of mine! This flamboyant, extravagant masterpiece is ironwork taken to new heights. It represents the pinnacle of Tijou's career, and it is impossible to imagine Hampton Court without the work of this French master blacksmith. It is not known where Jean Tijou came from, or where he went at the end of his life, but he arrived at Hampton Court at the same time as William and Mary in 1689, and immediately constructed an exquisite little balcony for the new queen.

The screen, constructed in 1690, has 12 panels, two each of six designs, depicting the emblems of England (the rose), Ireland (the harp), a thistle for Scotland, William and Mary's monogram, the garter star and the Fleur de Lys. It was originally intended for the East Front Garden but was still in Tijou's workshop years later in 1701, when William III's Privy Garden was nearing completion. The panels were then temporarily strung up into position between wooden poles at the end of the Privy Garden so that the king, sitting at his first floor window, could offer his opinion. He approved the screen but, to the gardeners' despair, asked for the newly planted garden to be lowered several feet to give a view of the Thames. The exhausted gardeners may have perhaps cursed the king, for just a few months later, in the adjacent Home Park, William fell from his favourite horse, Sorrel, as it stumbled on a mole hill. The king suffered a broken collarbone, fever set in and two weeks later he was dead. The unfortunate Tijou presented his unpaid bills to Queen Anne, but was never fully paid. Several years later he vanished, possibly back to his native France, leaving behind these fabulous screens. SG

Coronation spoon, 12th century

Silver, originally enamelled, re-gilded in the 1820s, engraved, pearl inset
Length 26.7 cm, weight 83.9 g
THE JEWEL HOUSE, TOWER OF LONDON

THIS ANCIENT SPOON, first recorded as part of the coronation regalia in 1349, is the oldest item in the Crown Jewels, and the only piece of royal goldsmiths' work to survive from the twelfth century. It survived destruction by the newly victorious Parliamentarians in 1649, when the medieval regalia were smashed, legendary jewels sold off and gold crown frames melted down for coinage in an anti-royalist orgy of destruction. Was the importance of this discreetly beautiful spoon overlooked somehow? It was bought for 16 shillings (its weight price) by Clement Kynnersley, a former keeper of the Royal Wardrobe. Clement kept it safe until the restoration of the monarchy, when he wisely handed it over to Charles II, and was reinstated in his old job, even though he had worked in the same role for Cromwell. It is debatable how this exquisite, finely engraved, double-lobed and pearl-studded spoon started life. Possibly it was the spoon

used to mix water and wine at Mass, or used perhaps at the Court of Henry II or Richard the Lionheart. Despite relatively humble beginnings, by the fourteenth century it was venerated as an ancient, holy object thought worthy of the task of anointing a new monarch. Anointing is the most sacred moment of a coronation, representing the transformation of the 'ordinary' person into a sovereign. The application of holy oil to the head, shoulders, breast and hands of the monarch is always performed by the Archbishop of Canterbury out of sight of the congregation. The Archbishop pours oil from the ampulla (a golden bottle shaped like an eagle) into the spoon, dips his fore and second fingers into its conveniently double-lobed bowl, and with blessings and prayers, anoints the monarch. Only then can they don the coronation robes and reappear, cleansed and purified, for the actual crowning. SDS

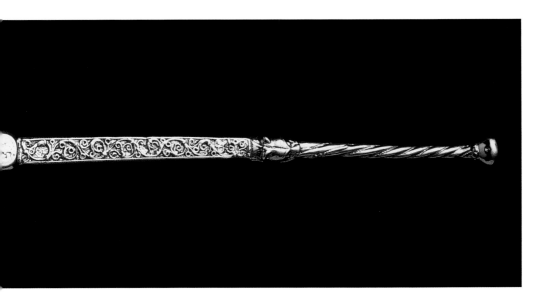

Wall and ceiling decoration, 1701

ANTONIO VERRIO *c.*1636–1707

Oil on plaster

LITTLE BANQUETING HOUSE, HAMPTON COURT PALACE (view by special arrangement)

I AM A CHAMPION of Verrio's riotous paintings, particularly these in William III's after-dinner den by the Thames, where he entertained his special friends. The fashion for Baroque mural paintings died out quickly, which is a shame, as the Baroque was, I think, far livelier than the more restrained neoclassical decorative ideas that followed. Verrio has used the slightly naughty, water-based stories from Ovid's *Metamorphoses* as his inspiration for this colourful, lively space filled with tales of the gods' love lives.

To the left of the fireplace, Arethusa is chased by lusty Altheus; to the right, Bacchus rescues the lovely Ariadne from her exile on Naxos. Elsewhere, pleasure-loving Pan pursues a gorgeous nymph, while Io is turned into a heifer. On the ceiling (shown left), Minerva, goddess of wisdom, and her all-seeing eye, presides over the arts and sciences. Around the edges of the painting are represent-ations of the four winds, the seasons and their associated signs of the zodiac. Nestled among them is a bust of William III, the whole com-ing together to say: 'Welcome to my private party, enjoy yourselves, live and love like the gods but don't forget who has made all this possible.' As part of the language of magnifi-cence of Hampton Court, the painting was intended to impress and dazzle. However, nineteenth-century 'Grace & Favour' resi-dents of the Little Banqueting House were not

so enthused, and for a long time these colourful scenes were obscured by two large bookcases. In 1864, a new tenant, Mrs Bailey, was shocked when she arrived at the unfurnished apartment. She protested to the Lord Chamberlain that the 'large undressed figures... should either be draped or clouded in some way to render them appropriate decorations for a drawing room'. Thank goodness he disagreed. BD

Lord Boston's Court coat, 1885

HENRY POOLE & SONS, LONDON
Wool with metal embroidery
KENSINGTON PALACE (on rotating display)

IN THE AUTUMN of 1885, the 25-year-old Lord Boston went to Henry Poole & Sons on Savile Row and ordered this glorious gold-embroidered, full dress second-class uniform (there were five classes, depending on one's status at Court). It cost what was then the colossal sum of £115, but he wore it proudly for the rest of his life. As the new sixth Baron Boston, he had recently been offered the prestigious post of Lord-in-Waiting to Queen Victoria, so this extravagant buy must have seemed like a good investment. He had his coat altered just a few months after he bought it, days before he kissed the hand of the queen at his official swearing in as Lord-in-Waiting. He had the neckline – and its expensive gold embroidery – cut down, probably to give him more room to breathe. Barely a year later, the post was offered to someone else, and Lord Boston's major concern, as revealed in correspondence with the Lord Chamberlain, was that he might never wear his flamboyant uniform again! Although he was re-offered the post, he declined, but he was allowed to continue wearing his full dress uniform at Court. And wear it he did, notably at several coronations over his lifetime. After the war, the stiff formality of Court presentations disappeared, and with it the need for full dress Court uniforms. By the 1960s, the glamorous but old-fashioned military and Court

uniforms were being sold in trendy used-clothing boutiques, like the famous 'I Was Lord Kitchener's Valet' on Carnaby Street. Appropriated by rock stars like Jimi Hendrix and a fashionable young set, the stuffy, braid-laden status symbols of the pre-war period were transformed into edgy, subversive fashion objects, best accessorised, of course, with an electric guitar. DM

Princess Margaret's menu book, 1996

KENSINGTON PALACE (not on display)

IT MAY LOOK UNEXCEPTIONAL, but the pencilled scribbles, restaurant French and nostalgic 1960s cuisine of this little menu book offer an endearing glimpse into Princess Margaret's later years at Kensington Palace. After her divorce from Lord Snowdon in 1978, the Princess continued to live alone in Apartment 1a, where during the swinging 60s she and Snowdon had entertained celebrities – from film stars and dancers to actors and singers. Margaret – beautiful, glamorous and fun-loving – and the handsome Snowdon were regarded as London's most chic couple, hosting dinner parties and costume balls, attending charity premieres and state banquets. So it's rather poignant to open this little book onto scenes from the very different life she was leading some 30 years later. Margaret requested from her personal chef a choice of three dishes for lunch, and three for dinner. I can imagine the menu book and a freshly sharpened pencil being presented with her breakfast tray; the Princess making the most of this modestly enjoyable task, lingering over the vol-au-vents, smoked chicken salads and 'Oeufs Arnold Bennett' (haddock omelette – a favourite of the novelist Arnold Bennett) before marking her choice with a cross. Sometimes there is a break in routine, and we see the classic 1960s-style selections crossed through with her handwritten instruction: 'Picnic for four for the ballet, cold ham etc'. Or occasionally a request for good English

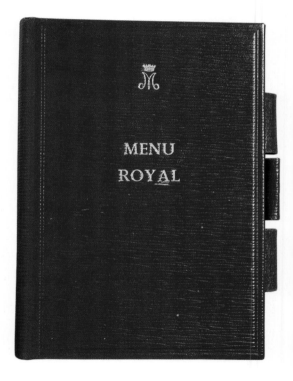

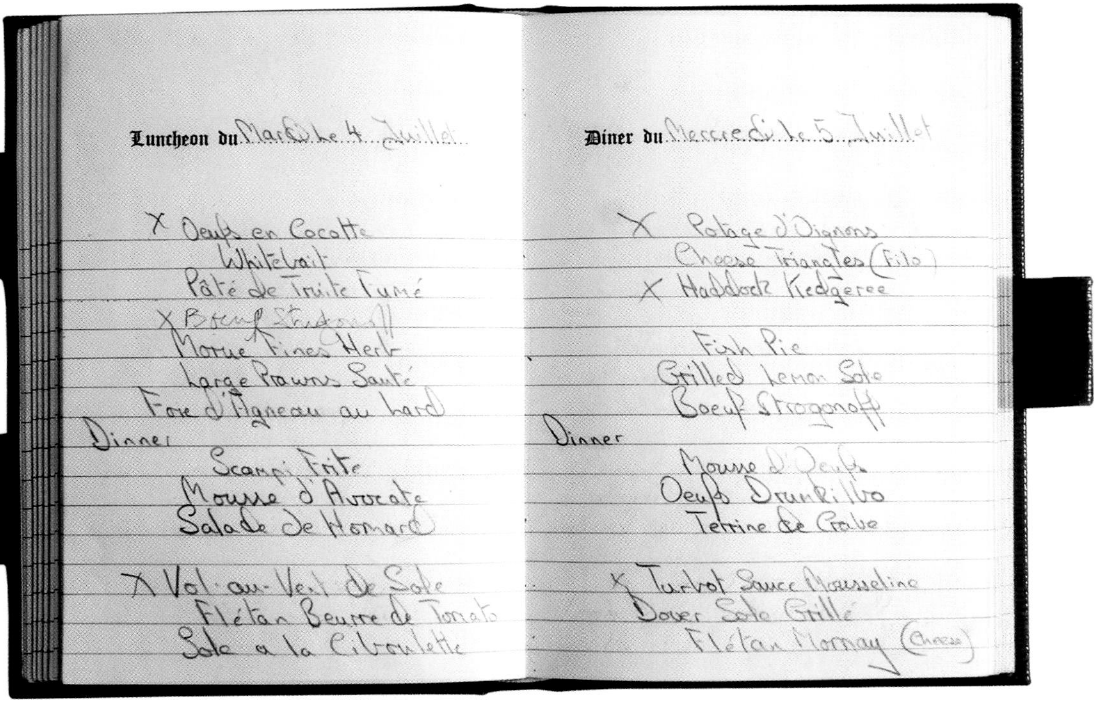

Luncheon du Mardi Le 4 Juillet

X Oeufs en Cocotte
   Whitebait
   Pâté de Truite Fumé
X Boeuf Stroganoff
   Morue Fines Herb
   Large Prawns Sauté
   Foie d'Agneau au Lard

Dinner
   Scampi Frite
   Mousse d'Avocate
   Salade De Homard

X Vol·au·Vent de Sole
   Flétan Beurre de Tomato
   Sole a la Ciboulette

Diner du Mercredi Le 5 Juillet

X Potage d'Oignons
   Cheese Triangles (Filo)
X Haddock Kedgeree

   Fish Pie
   Grilled Lemon Sole
   Boeuf Stroganoff

Dinner
   Mousse d'Oeufs
   Oeufs Drumkilbo
   Terrine de Crabe

X Turbot Sauce Mousseline
   Dover Sole Grillé
   Flétan Mornay (Cheese)

comfort food: 'Roast beef and Yorkshire Pudding'. I haven't decoded all the entries yet: 'Oeufs Drumkilbo' mystified me until I discovered it was a cold pressed mould of chopped eggs and seafood, such a firm favourite of the Queen Mother's that after her death it was never served in the royal household again. It's lovely to see it crop up so often in the menu belonging to her daughter. MD

The Family of Henry VIII, *c.*1545

UNKNOWN ARTIST
Oil on canvas, 1695 x 3569 cm
HAMPTON COURT PALACE

THIS IS A MOST remarkable portrait of Henry's family. No doubt hung where the Court and foreign visitors could not fail to see it, this luminous painting served to extol Henry's dynasty. As the buildings curator at Hampton Court Palace, I find intriguing the way the architecture of this imagined sixteenth-century interior is used to convey subtle, and not so subtle, messages to the viewer. Firstly, this is a classical, not medieval interior, suggesting a monarch of huge sophistication and learning. It gives an idea of the way Henry thought of architecture as providing a platform from which to play his role as king. Secondly, the hierarchy is crystal clear. Framed in the central scene under a lavish canopy of state is an impossible grouping of people: Henry, his precious son and male heir Edward, and Jane Seymour, Edward's mother (who died due to complications from his birth). On either side, separated by columns and standing off the rich central carpet, are his two daughters by previous marriages, Mary, to our left, and Elizabeth. The architecture both serves to frame that composition and make it more magnificent, but it also works to divide the focus of the picture, so that when one's gaze shifts from the central group, Mary and Elizabeth come into focus, then the real world of London and Whitehall Palace glimpsed in the background. Further back, there are two Tudor fools: Will Somers, with the monkey, was Henry's court jester; the other is probably Jane, Mary's fool and a member of her household. Their inclusion was probably intended as a reminder of the human weaknesses of kings and princes. KR

The Spitalfields mantua, 1750–55

Brocaded silk
Petticoat 92 x 219 cm, bodice 38 cm shoulder to waist
KENSINGTON PALACE (on rotating display)

STUNNING, AN INCREDIBLY rare survival and utterly absurd! The wearer could do absolutely *nothing* in this frock except stand still, her rigid stays (similar to a corset) keeping her upright for hours in the monarch's presence. Any physical activity more taxing than some light dancing was impossible, which was the whole point. Strangely, mantuas (an ensemble of a bodice with a train attached that is lifted over hoops to expose the petticoat underneath), although extravagant in design, were originally an informal style of dress. By the mid-eighteenth century, however, they were worn exclusively at Court. After hours of standing attendance, the wearer would be 'released' rather than undressed by her maids. They would dismantle the outfit bit by bit, undoing the stomacher from the bodice, removing the washable parts (lace cuffs and undergarments) and untying the huge whalebone or cane hoops that held the petticoat out on either side of the body.

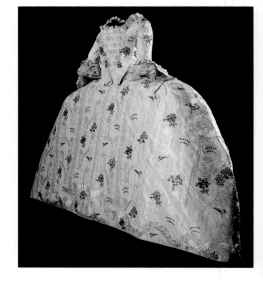

This mantua, the earliest in our collection, was made in the famous Spitalfields area of east London, where families of weavers created gorgeous brocaded silk. The fabric in this example is very complex, as the flower motifs are woven into it rather than embroidered onto it, and the background silk is highly decorative. The shape and size of the hoops changed over time, but mantuas were still worn at Court for 40 years after they ceased to be fashionable. Eventually, pilloried by satirical cartoonists and the cause of increasing congestion, they were dispensed with by the extremely fashionable George IV in 1820. MD

Stained-glass window, late 15th–18th century

Scene with knight: 40 x 61 cm

CHAPEL OF ST JOHN THE EVANGELIST, WHITE TOWER, TOWER OF LONDON

THE STAINED GLASS in St John's Chapel was once part of the collection of Horace Walpole, the great eighteenth-century antiquarian and collector. Most of it was originally from Walpole's Round Drawing Room at Strawberry Hill, and came to the Tower after it was bought in the great auction of his collection in 1842. The stained glass was installed in St John's Chapel in the late nineteenth century. These fragments span four centuries, and they reflect Walpole's eclectic taste. They are welcome reminders that St John's Chapel once had its own stained glass, painted with the Virgin and Child, the Holy Trinity and St John the Evangelist, installed after 1240, and long since disappeared. We can only imagine the entire scenes of which Walpole's fragments were once a part. This dynamic knight, who probably dates from the late fifteenth century, is a particular favourite of mine. The flamboyant plume on his helmet, his dashing scimitar and the elaborate silver-sulphide yellow 'gilded' plate armour and shield are beautifully rendered by the most skillful of glass painters. The knight raises his eyes upwards, an arm shielding his anxious face. He twists his body around to look at something above a tomb-like structure behind him from which the lid has slipped. What could he be looking at in such alarm? I think that he is a Roman soldier, guarding Jesus's tomb. He has fallen to his knees in astonishment, witnessing the Resurrection of Christ. We shall never know exactly what the knight is staring at – it is not recorded what this scene shows, or where it came from, and now he kneels alone, marooned in a sea of white glass. The heightened emotion of the scene contrasts dramatically with the monumental, serene Norman architecture of the chapel, making it especially poignant. JS

Mercury Presenting The Liberal Arts to Apollo and Diana, 1628

GERRIT VAN HONTHORST 1590–1656
Oil, 357 x 640 cm
THE QUEEN'S STAIRCASE, HAMPTON COURT PALACE

THIS PAINTING IS WONDERFUL because, while it does not show an actual Stuart masque, it creates a great sense of what it would have been like to attend one of these fabulously extravagant, early seventeenth-century Court entertainments. There was singing, acting, music, dialogue, amazing costume and, above all, splendid 'special effects'. This painting shows an apparently miraculous 'floating cloud' descending from above, which would have allowed the actors their dramatic entrance. Sitting on the cloud is the king himself, Charles I, in the red toga; and his feisty French wife, Henrietta Maria, is seated next to him.

On one level, the picture tells the story of Mercury, who is seen leading the Liberal Arts over the Alps and into England into the presence of Apollo (the king). The message being conveyed is that the reign of Charles I has been a golden age for the arts – challenging fashionable Italy for the first time. However, there is a personal story inherent in the picture also. Look at the powerful gaze being exchanged between the two men. The sitter playing the character of Mercury (see the wings on his helmet) is the Duke of Buckingham, who was the favourite of Charles's father, James I, and who had a strange, manipulative hold over both father and son. He was deeply unpopular due to the powerful influence he seemed to have over both kings: James I was bisexual and adored his 'Steenie', as he called Buckingham, and Charles I treated him as something of a father figure. And that is Buckingham's wife next to him (bare-breastedness was not uncommon in Stuart Court masques). The two men gaze intently at each other, neither of them paying much heed to their neglected spouses. LW

Norman Hartnell.

Designs for peeresses' caps of state, for the 1953 coronation

NORMAN HARTNELL 1901–1979
Pencil and watercolour on paper
KENSINGTON PALACE (not on display)

WHEN PRINCESS ELIZABETH married in 1947, the press speculation over the design of her dress reached fever pitch. Royal couturier, Norman Hartnell, was forced to whitewash his studio window to keep prying eyes out, despite a 24-hour security watch on the building. When the shimmering gown was revealed on the day of the wedding, it caused a sensation. Hartnell, who had started his career as a theatre designer, never looked back. The spectacular gown he designed for the Queen for her 1953 coronation, embroidered theatrically with emblems of the Commonwealth, was hailed as a triumph. However, combining fashion with formality was not always easy, as these funny, rather charming little sketches that we acquired in 2005 reveal. In his autobiography, Hartnell writes at length (extraordinary length!) about designing coronation dresses and robes, and it is clear these caps of state proved more troublesome for him than the rest of his 'coronation collection' put together. Caps of state and coronets (which are similar to crowns) are carried at a coronation by members of the aristocracy, who don them at the climax when the monarch is crowned. Such a dramatic moment requires dignified and simple headgear, and Hartnell's attempts to create something theatrical and stylish using traditional red velvet and ermine did not fit the bill on this occasion. None of these designs was produced, and eventually a much simpler cap was approved. DM

Portrait of Christian IV, King of Denmark, 1640

KAREL VAN MANDER 1606–1670

Oil on canvas, 231.7 x 169.8 cm

Limewood frame by Grinling Gibbons, c.1699

KING'S EATING ROOM, HAMPTON COURT PALACE

WE KNOW THAT King William III chose this portrait to grace his new dining room in 1700. But why? Christian IV was the brother of Anne of Denmark, who was married to James I, and he was invited to England in 1606 to be royally entertained at Court. It is the account of these revelries, recorded by the courtier and writer, John Harrington, that draw me to this painting and to the boisterous character of the man himself. This life-size portrait captures the Danish king formally, but we should remember that this is the man who allegedly insisted that Danish beer be brewed to be the strongest in the world. John Harrington, and indeed the English

Court, must have treasured his visit: 'We had women and indeed wine too, in such plenty that it would have astonished each sober beholder. Our feasts were magnificent and the two royal guests did most lovingly embrace each other at table. I think the Dane has strangely wrought on our good English nobles, for those I could never get to taste good liquor, now follow the fashion and wallow in beastly delight. Ladies abandon their sobriety and are seen to roll about in intoxication.' Meanwhile, back in Denmark, Christian is witnessed (by an English ambassador) drinking 35 toasts during a meal before collapsing in his chair and being carried off to a dark room. So I don't think it was an accident that William, who appreciated a joke while reinforcing his Stuart ancestry, placed this portrait here in his dining room, where his great great uncle would feel most at home. BD

Tankard, late 18th–early 19th century

Pewter

ARCHAEOLOGICAL STORE, TOWER OF LONDON (view by special arrangement)

MUCH OF WHAT we have in the archaeological store at the Tower might be considered rubbish – but it's interesting rubbish! So many seemingly humdrum items that possess, however, a surprising poignancy: buttons, bowls, bits of pipe, commonplace debris dropped from pockets or thrown out over centuries by people who lived and worked within the Tower walls. This tankard is one of two dug up in the 1990s near to the Bell Tower at the end of Mint Street, where my office is today, and where there once stood a tavern called the *Stone Kitchen* (shown in this watercolour by T.H. Shepherd). At the end of the eighteenth century, the Tower was a bustling

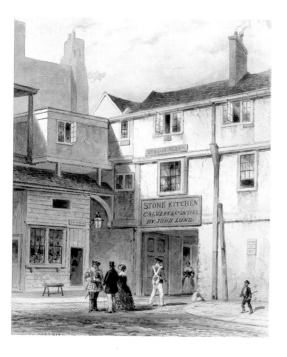

industrial and military centre. Besides the visitors to the Crown Jewels, Armouries and Royal Menagerie, there was the Royal Mint, a garrison and a body of Yeoman Warders, with plenty of thirsty and hungry people to service. There were several pubs on site; we assume the *Kitchen* was the favoured haunt of Yeoman Warder Francis Dobson, who joined the Yeoman Body in 1791, for it is his name, along with the tavern's, that are inscribed on both tankards. For good measure, his initials are also engraved on the thumb rests. I can imagine these tankards hanging behind the bar, ready for YW Dobson to appear. He died in April 1810 and was buried at the Tower chapel of St Peter ad Vincula – just one of the ordinary people who lived, worked and died an unremarkable death here, alongside those who more famously lost their heads on Tower Green. And just like today's Yeoman Warders, YW Dobson enjoyed a pint in his local at the end of a hard day! SDS

The Holland Monument, 15th century

Alabaster and stone

CHAPEL OF ST PETER AD VINCULA, TOWER OF LONDON

JOHN HOLLAND, CREATED Duke of Exeter in 1444, was Constable of the Tower of London from 1420 until his death in 1447. It is perhaps fitting that his imposing tomb's final resting place should be the Tower, although he had intended to lie in everlasting grandeur in the church of the Royal Hospital of St Katherine, next door (his tomb eventually came to the Chapel of St Peter after the church was destroyed). John, a great soldier, distinguished himself fighting for Henry V in France, and was a councillor for the child-king, Henry VI. He was rewarded for his loyalty with the appointment of Constable for life. John was a man of lavish tastes, as this extravagant tomb indicates, although he was always a little financially embarrassed. He married three wealthy widows to maintain him in style, one or two of whom are also interred here. Next to the alabaster effigy of Holland, his head resting on a crowned helm, is wife number one, Anne, his favourite. The second figure could be his third wife, also called Anne, who outlived him; or his sister Constance, as he wished to be buried with both. The stone tomb canopy is beautifully carved with censing and trumpeting angels, and with lively little hunting and folk-tale scenes, which are great favourites of mine. One vignette shows a goose hanging a fox by the neck! Holland's will shows that the tomb was part of a chantry chapel where he provided money for four priests to say prayers and celebrate Masses to speed his and his wives' and sister's souls through Purgatory. Holland may have encountered a slight hitch on his way Heavenward. Tradition has it that either he or his son – who became Constable after him – devised the hideous torture device, 'the rack', chillingly known in the sixteenth century as 'The Duke of Exeter's Daughter'. JS

Queen Charlotte's State Bed, 1772 onwards

JOHN YENN (?) architect, PHOEBE WRIGHT embroiderer,
ROBERT CAMPBELL upholsterer
Height 396 cm, width 223 cm, length 233 cm
HAMPTON COURT PALACE (view by special arrangement)

THIS IS PROBABLY the last in the line of an extraordinary phe-
nomenon – the royal state bed. These huge, lavish structures,
an alternative royal setting to a 'throne', enjoyed their heyday
from the time of the early Stuarts to the Hanoverians, King
George III and Queen Charlotte. By the time this bed – the
most magnificent of all – was finished for the queen to use
at Windsor, the Court was changing. *Levées* and *couchées* – in
which the monarch was dressed and undressed in the
presence of several courtiers – no longer took place, and the
bedchamber became a more private space. It is unlikely
that Charlotte ever used this bed, let alone lay beneath the pale
cream silken cover gazing up at the exquisite tester dome
which had been made solely for her delight. (George and
Charlotte had other, less magnificent beds from which
emerged their 15 children.) The bed is an extraordinary creation – a mixture of formal, classical architecture (George III's
favourite architect, William Chambers, may have had a hand
in the design), covered with thousands of botanically accurate,
embroidered flowers, possibly designed by the royal artist,
Mary Moser. The queen privately commissioned these enormous pieces of needlework from Mrs Wright's 'School for
Embroidering Females'. Charlotte, who liked to dedicate herself to charitable causes, visited this school for orphan girls
and took a close personal interest in its 'women's work'. By
the time of Queen Victoria's reign, this monumental but essentially 'useless' bed had found its way to Hampton Court.
Victoria opened the palace to the public for the first time and
the bed quickly became one of its great attractions, and has
remained here ever since. SE

The Wine Fountain, 2010

Recreation, inspired by a detail from
Field of Cloth of Gold, unknown artist, *c.*1545
Painted and gilded bronze and timber
BASE COURT, HAMPTON COURT PALACE

HENRY VIII'S WINE FOUNTAIN, depicted in the painting *Field of Cloth of Gold*, is one of the most playful objects he ever commissioned for the entertainment of his Court. The painting (also at Hampton Court) commemorates the fortnight-long extravaganza in 1520 when Henry travelled to Guines (near Calais) to meet, joust, wrestle and occasionally talk politics with Francis I of France. The fountain, which flowed with red and white wine, and claret (the sixteenth-century word for rosé), was just one opulent detail in the extraordinary temporary camp that was set up, at the heart of which was a complete Italianate palace made from painted canvas and timber. We took a gamble in recreating it, since the artist may not even have seen the original, but we have demonstrated that the fountain he painted actually works when translated into a three-dimensional, 4-metre-high object. Ours, probably like the original, is of timber painted to look like marble, with elements such as the gilded lion heads and the frieze drawn from surviving Tudor decoration around the palace. And it flows with red and white wine. So often Henry VIII is associated with beheadings and a ferocious temper. Our fountain communicates the message that Hampton Court was the opposite of that. It was a pleasure palace where Henry entertained and spoilt his guests. Of course,

he was always trying to influence and control them, but he would seduce them first with food, music, good hunting, dancing and lots of alcohol! Our fountain's bright colours may come as a bit of a shock at first sight, but they highlight the extent to which the palace colours have become muted and mellow with age. Five hundred years ago, the brickwork was painted bright red, with the mortar picked out in white. For me, the fountain is a wonderful reminder of just how dramatic and colourful Henry's palaces and entertainments really were. KR

Royal puzzle maps, *c.*1762–66

Cabinet mahogany, English
KEW PALACE (presented to HRP and the V&A Museum of Childhood by The Art Fund)

THESE PUZZLE MAPS, some of the earliest ever made, belonged to the children of King George III and Queen Charlotte. Cut out by hand, they are the original 'jigsaws', as they became known in the Victorian period. Their pieces follow the boundaries of maps from early atlases (there is still no Australasia or 'wild west' of America), making them an educational challenge to put together. As a royal object, it is very modest: a plain mahogany cabinet – in fact, two stuck together, with 16 little drawers inside, each with the name of a country scrawled in pencil on the front, and each containing a puzzle map. It also includes some rather less well-made puzzles – one of Europe with its countries labelled by a young child – which must have been an exercise by one of the royal children. The cabinet belonged to the much-loved royal governess, Lady Charlotte Finch, who brought up and helped educate the royal children at Kew and elsewhere. She passed this cabinet on to her niece, who thoughtfully pinned a note to it explaining its provenance for future generations. Without this, it might have remained an impersonal object and not recognised as having been the plaything of the future King George IV, who went on to rule over many of the lands that were mapped onto his childhood jigsaws. SE

Queen Victoria's split drawers, *c.*1900

Linen
Waist 135 cm, length 57 cm
KENSINGTON PALACE (on rotating display)

SUCH AN INTIMATE piece of clothing brings home to me the physicality of the elderly queen. By the end of her life, this 5-feet-tall, formerly petite woman was extremely stout, a result of eating too much, too fast – she was often reprimanded for 'scoffing' in her youth. This is a pair of her drawers, which were made without a gusset. This style was fashionable when Victoria was a young woman and she stayed with it throughout her life, despite the fact that trends changed over the course of the nineteenth century and, whilst still unseen, drawers became tighter, showier and even made from coloured fabric. Victoria bought her fine linen knickers in batches, and they were all painstakingly numbered and embroidered with her monogram. There is a tradition within the British royal family of distributing garments on the death of a monarch – including these very personal items. Because of this, survival of royal clothing is patchy, so we are very happy to have these. They must have been treasured for years by the descendants of one of her household, and we purchased them at auction. Victoria's utilitarian undergarments were never to be seen by anyone except her most intimate servants – but I enjoy the fact that they still had to be emblazoned with a crown! MD

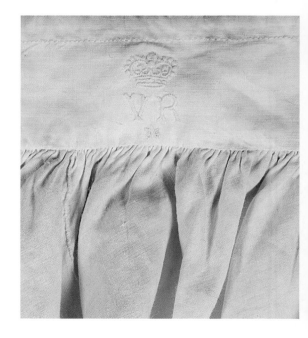

King's Grand Staircase painting, mid-1720s

WILLIAM KENT 1685–1748
Oil on canvas, wood and plaster
KENSINGTON PALACE

I HAVE BEEN FASCINATED by this staircase ever since my first visit to Kensington Palace, because of the mysterious figures on its walls and ceiling. The work was created in the 1720s by William Kent, the bumptious young painter who was commissioned for the job – to everyone's surprise – by George I. Kent used people from the royal household as his sitters, and I like to imagine him, the outsider, choreographing the Court to fulfil his vision.

There are 45 people in the painting (including Kent himself), and I see it as an enormous puzzle. I do think that they are all real people, and that it might be possible to identify each of them, but in the four years I have been researching the staircase, I've only identified 12 to my satisfaction, using alternative portraits and court records to build the case for each sitter. So who have we got? The boy in green is Peter the Wild Boy, a feral child found in the woods of Germany and brought to Court as a kind of pet. The man standing behind him is Dr John Arbuthnot, medical doctor and satirist, who tried to teach Peter how to speak. Mustapha and Mohammed, George I's two Turkish valets, are there. Mohammed wears a blue cloak and stands in profile; Mustapha is to his right, in the background, with a white beard and a turban. On the ceiling is William Kent himself (on the left, in a reddish brown coat and turban), along with his two assistants and the actress, Elizabeth Butler, said to be his mistress. The staircase may not be a masterpiece – in fact, some would say that Kent never managed the human figure very successfully. But this was Kent's first big break; he went on to become the best-known designer of the Georgian age. I like the staircase because of its stories, and because it is a brilliant, endlessly fascinating mystery. LW

Lock, 1690s–1700

Brass outer box, steel mechanism, engraved
KING'S INNER CLOSET, HAMPTON COURT PALACE

WHEN PEOPLE WANDER through the grand rooms of the State Apartments, they may rarely cast their eyes downwards and notice the great brass locks adorning the doors. Nor are they likely to be aware of the delightful fact that many were made by Mr Josiah Key. These were prestigious items, and expensive to make, so just by looking at a particular lock and its lavish decoration it is possible to locate oneself exactly within the palace and know the importance of the room the lock belongs to. The locks made for the State Apartments of William III and Mary II are known as rim locks, which means they are fixed externally to the door, so in theory they are removeable and can be reattached to any door, unlike modern mortice locks which are buried inside the wood itself. The rim lock is essentially a plain box of brass, with a varying array of knobs and decorative elements attached to it for aesthetic appeal. This is one of the finest, giving access to one of the most important rooms in the palace, and it bears the royal cipher 'W & M' (for William and Mary) set in an elegant surround. What we cannot see is the mechanism, a wonder in its own right. It would have been made from an early form of steel, the latest technology honed from gun manufacture (locks and weapons were often made by the same craftsmen). Another clever touch: the mechanism inside the lock is hard wearing, while the key, which could be replaced more easily and cheaply, is of softer alloy. LP

Self-portrait of Artemisia Gentileschi as La Pittura, 1638–39

ARTEMISIA GENTILESCHI 1593–1652
Oil on canvas, 98.6 x 75.2 cm
HAMPTON COURT PALACE

AN ASTONISHING IMAGE of a seventeenth-century woman, this is one of the most arresting paintings hanging at the palace today. For many years the female artist, Artemisia, was largely ignored by art historians, but within the last 30 years she has attracted the attention of filmmakers, novelists, gallery curators, historians and most particularly, feminist art historians – as much for her life as her work. But even without a background knowledge of Artemisia, there is something very different and special about this painting when compared with the work of her contemporaries. She has portrayed herself as the emblematic figure of Painting personified (*La Pittura*) as it was conceived in the late sixteenth century. In choosing *La Pittura* – a female ideal – Artemisia had a distinct advantage over her male rivals. However, Artemisia also portrays herself as a working artist, not stiffly posed amongst the standard symbols. What is immediately striking is her pose. She is absorbed in the moment, not looking out at us, the viewer, as the subjects of self-portraits generally did at this time. And she is leaning to catch her image in a momentary way that makes the painting incredibly dynamic, as if she is painting sweeping brushstrokes on a large canvas. This is significant, as large paintings – often stories from the Bible or history – required more skill and were expensive to commission. Her pose causes her pinned hair to fall out of place, and around her neck a small golden mask is just discernible. These are the 'props' for the emblem of *La Pittura* – a theatrical mask to indicate imitation, dishevelled hair revealing a passionate temperament, and a bound mouth – simply closed here – representing the mute quality of the visual arts. To paint oneself in this way was to make a rather radical statement, one that we have only come to appreciate fully almost 400 years after its creation. SE

Edward VII's baby shoes, 1841

Red silk velvet, rabbit fur, silver thread, leather soles
Length 13 cm
KENSINGTON PALACE (on rotating display)

MOTHERS INVARIABLY HAVE a soft spot for their babies' shoes, and many preserve them lovingly for years. Queen Victoria was no exception; she saved these tiny shoes, which were made for her eldest son, Edward, Prince of Wales, born 9 November 1841. She must have sighed over them in later years when Edward's extravagant lifestyle and numerous affairs with society beauties were causing his parents so much concern. Poor Edward (or Bertie, as he was known to his family) felt outshone by his witty and intelligent elder sister, the Princess Royal, and struggled with the strict education that Prince Albert demanded for his children. This put huge pressure on their relationship, before Bertie rebelled and abandoned himself to a socialite lifestyle. Edward was always beautifully dressed as an adult, and I like to imagine that his interest in fashion and style might have begun at a young age. He must have enjoyed wearing these princely slippers made of red silk velvet, trimmed with white rabbit (echoing the velvet and ermine of royal robes) and delicately embroidered with silver

thread. They are in very good condition, although the soles show some signs of wear; but they were probably only worn indoors. Family was very important to Queen Victoria. Although she wasn't terribly fond of babies (she once famously described them as looking like little frogs), she enjoyed her children once they could walk and talk. She kept shoes belonging to all of her nine children, and we even have a pair of her own, treasured by her mother the Duchess of Kent and now in the Royal Dress Collection at Kensington Palace. AK

First published in 2011 by
Scala Publishers Ltd
Northburgh House
10 Northburgh Street
London EC1V 0AT
www.scalapublishers.com

In association with Historic Royal Palaces
www.hrp.org.uk

ISBN: 978 1 85759 677 9

Editor: Sandra Pisano
Designer: Nigel Soper
Historic Royal Palaces editor: Sarah Kilby
Printed in Singapore

10 9 8 7 6 5 4 3 2 1

ACKNOWLEDGEMENTS

The Historic Royal Palaces (HRP) publications team, Sarah
Kilby, Susan Mennell and Annie Heron would like to thank
members of HRP staff and others who have contributed to
the preparation of this book. The costume photography
would not have been possible without the dedicated work
of our expert textile conservators: Anne-Marie Britton,
Christine Housden, Maria Jordan, Kaori Motaung and
Helen Slade, who prepared fragile, precious garments for
the camera. Photo shoots in historic environments always
require the co-operation of the wider team, so many
thanks to Yeoman Warders at the Tower of London, State
Apartment Warders at Hampton Court Palace and the
warding staff at Kensington Palace. And thank you to the
photographers themselves, Robin and Ian Forster, who
produce brilliant results in often testing circumstances!

Historic Royal PALACES

Historic Royal Palaces is the
independent charity that looks
after the Tower of London,
Hampton Court Palace, the
Banqueting House, Kensington
Palace and Kew Palace. We help
everyone explore the story of
how monarchs and people have
shaped society, in some of the
greatest palaces ever built.

We receive no funding from the
Government or the Crown, so
we depend on the support of
our visitors, members, donors,
volunteers and sponsors.

FRONT/BACK COVER:
Unknown artist,
*The Family of Henry
VIII* (detail), *c.*1545
(see pages 48–49)

FRONTISPIECE:
Unknown artist,
Field of Cloth of Gold
(detail), *c.*1540–50
(see pages 66–67)